THE OPPOSITE OF LIGHT

THE OPPOSITE
OF LIGHT

POEMS

KIMBERLY GREY

WINNER OF THE LEXI RUDNITSKY FIRST BOOK PRIZE IN POETRY

A KAREN & MICHAEL BRAZILLER BOOK
PERSEA BOOKS / NEW YORK

Persea Books, Inc.
277 Broadway
New York, NY 10007

Library of Congress Cataloging-in-Publication Data
Names: Grey, Kimberly, 1985–
Title: The opposite of light : poems / Kimberly Grey.
Description: First edition. | New York : Persea Books, 2016. | "A Karen & Michael Braziller book."
Identifiers: LCCN 2015034510 | ISBN 9780892554713 (original trade pbk. : alk. paper)
Classification: LCC PS3607.R49935 A6 2016 | DDC 811/.6—dc23
LC record available at http://lccn.loc.gov/2015034510

First edition
Printed in the United States of America
Designed by Rita Lascaro

for John

CONTENTS

[contraria contrariis curantur]

HIPPOCRATES

ONE

Invention

Built your truss, built your small back,
all I could muster, all cheek and luck.
Built your hum to crescendo and bucked
it suddenly. You are not usual. Built
your not usual, your poor blue, your quiet
monkish heart. Globes came and constructed
themselves around you. Built your shucks,
your shakes, your one size fits my size,
part luster, part strum. Built your brightly
and bejeezus. God himself could not
have built your bejeezus. Built your little
horse and gallop, learned to leave
and return to you, unfinished sun. Built
your troubadour, your *je t'adore*, your door-
to-door salesman mouth. Perfection is
the unsaid lover of approximation, built you
perfect and guilty—your war and glimmer
dirty on the floor. If I am building you, I have
forgiven you. If I am building you, we are halfway
to a boat that whirs *You first into the blue.*
Built your scruff and scrap, your once twice
three times electric body. Your head may
be dying but I built it dying, built the light
around the light around the light. Marvelous
contraption, before the solstice I will fill you
in with sky. Built your bumble to bumble,
your pop to pop, your hurt, however it hurts,
to hurt. God bless your hot bones. God bless
your drunken hope. Built you to break continually,
as everything breaks continually, as a circle
of words, as Duchamp's nude, naked (your nouns
showing). Built you until I finished you,

and you finished me too. Unraveled me like
the flight of a thousand bramblings. *Oh Monsieur,
Oh Madame,* built your wild wild, your sprout
and gasp! your beautiful undid me done.

Mentally, we are in love
    with each other, or chemically,
however they say, our minds
    with minds of their own and
nothing as old-fashioned as making
    a lover with a rib. But how do we
keep from moving forward too
    quickly and what do we do
with all the preciousness and time-
    lessness and sadness? Even history
can't keep us. We keep inventing
    newfangled ways to be in the world.
Just yesterday I overheard a husband
    say *Give me a vacuum to clean*
our orange sky. Imagine an antique
    computer. Imagine a zoomed-in,
pixelated hurt. Let's be vegan.
    Let's drive a Prius. Let's find a robot
to make our bed and bring us tea.
    My dear, I promise to homeschool
you if you homeschool me. I am
    a 21st–century wife. Tonight I'll touch
you in some otherworldly way
    and we'll copyright it, YouTube it,
tell the general public this is our way
    of being modern. We know all
the proper ways to evolve. Once
    we lived by the sundial,
the wristwatch, the harvest's gold. Now
    we are learning to breathe in bytes.
We are tracing the light waves
    and brain waves back to some

historically complex time. We are
  closing the bedroom door. Still
there's a drop of blue light. But no high-tech
  way to say *You're mine.* No way to love
each other but with these ancient bodies.

Epithalamium *ABC*

*A*nd with these rings we'll learn to gather sighs, too, over and under bridges
wherever we find ourselves, wound-up and hurried. A wet braid all the way down
my back. Our bodies hard then soft and hard. Zip and bone. And the eggs
from the market reminding us that marriage is yellow, the edges

Burnt. Also, that we are toy cars, electric and modern. That we'll drive each other
crazy and spill over. November is deciduous. That's when we met, when we marry.
We'll learn to be quiet. That we are quiet. That we can't be quiet. Yes I'll take you.
I'll eat your pea soup. Vacuum the bedroom floor. This

Cicatrice that opens and closes, it's yours, mine for always. Yes I agree to have it, hold
it up to the light, stroke it in darkness. However jagged. And if it needs fixing, I do
have hammer, screws. I'll take you to the zoo, let the jargonelle grow, be always wife
to your husband, which is loving, learning to suffer in the same ways. Mostly, I

Do.

If X equals Y there is less than an island
between them. If X equals sky then there is
almost room for Y in the concave of X's body.
If X is burned, Y is also burned. But curiously,
with a pretty red. If X has a figure, Y grows
fainter in the sun. If X has a figure, Y is doomed.
Don't look back now. There is a blithe and pithy
future before us. X is pouring out a better life. Y
is smoking a cigar. How could we leave them alone?
X is standing in the rain. Y is painting X standing
in the rain. This is called an artful gesture. How else
to remember the hurt map we've marked? Once
there was a brush fire and everything burned
but one single weed. Y loves this story. Y tells it to X
but X can only hear that we are dropping bombs
somewhere and each shadow is just a faint clue.
If the top of the piano shined any brighter in the sun
there would be no music. Or only music. Maybe X
dreamt Y. Maybe Y is lit up. Maybe Y glows with X.
There is a country of possible ways to love another.
X is full of awe. Y has some. Both are full of history
and hipbones and everything we don't know yet.
Between X and Y there is a whispering of *I will keep
you I will keep you I will keep you*. A sighed counting,
of any combination of lovers, who are not us.

Reverie

When I wanted you bird,
you bared.
Unzipped and high, you grasped
the bedpost and begged,
Isn't this all for truth?
I ran through the snow
and you were there.
You said let's love like the lotus
but how does the lotus love?
The storm licked us
wet. I wanted a lovemonger.
You were a warmonger, a stingy
color, a west. When I say
I'm going
east, you say screw me
in half. Darling, this isn't violence.
You are more than deliberate.
The wind blows me this way.
I am figuring you out.

Somehow, We are a We

So many beautiful, manageable heads. If only we were
allowed a hundred different joys. What a radical idea.
No goodness will get you far. Your loveliness is measured
by the number of poor things you've dazzled. Add in
an old city ruin, and some translated light, which is
foreign and sounds cool, but cannot be understood.
Goodness is contrived. No one wants it. It's before
breakfast and already our hearts have gone bad.
Yesterday I watched two birds fight over the same
blue square of sky. The philosophers say if you take
something you don't love in your arms and unhurt it,
you will be happy. But we are not happy. Everything
electrical is not light. All over there are crowds
of people waiting to be caressed. Every bed in the world
was manufactured for just a few. We are magnolia
white, spoon light, left-over flight. We are spiny
and unforgivable. But it's good to ache and be wise for it.
You come back in the door that I've walked out of.
It's ceremonial. It's revolving. The back of your beautiful
head. Your hands are here, I can't tell where, but it is
the best kind of uncertainty. Happiness is when every
thing inside you goes out and comes back in, newly.

OF NEWNESS

I could
say kiss
          me, I am
a paper
          bird, I am
          brand new
and still
we'd be
          something
          archaic.

Conjugating

         If lovers are
swallowing the nation of each other,
         what haven't they
already swallowed? (I thought about
         this once, as you
bridled a horse and a bird flew
         into your mouth).
We have not minded, are not minding,
         the problems
that time brings. It was in Omaha where
         I said *Until you are god*
again I am god. This is when I learned
         you are not
impressed by me, that I am not
         impressing
or damming, that nothing has bloomed
         enough for us to eat
and be full of it. If the heart is a heart
         or was a heart,
it will be continue to be a heart. Time says
         it, the wife is wived,
the husband husbanded and there's nothing
         we can do about it.
When Stein wrote *pain soup*, she might
         have meant this:
that we are doomed, dooming, dumb.
         That when I promised
you time, I promised nothing but the notion
         of it. That what we are
right now is shinery—rough flecks; not light
         but light's potential
to change us into that thing we never were

before, that we are
not now. So much time piled up inside us
both, perhaps one
day we'll understand: why it hurts to be here,
and there, and then.

What people we have been who don't know a whole, we
never thought *[to arrive kindly]*
to the ends of each other. Yes *[you burn me]*
into a *[more finely shaped]* half and yes I'd call it straining, this incomplete
language we never finish. It's exhausting *[the mind like a mountain]*—
and sometimes puzzling, sometimes depressing.
Maybe disillusionment means we're living, maybe
this is how everyone is living, *[yes many
and beautiful things]*, more beautiful than us, *[make a way with the mouth]*
because a mouth can carry hurt the way a body cannot.
[Knees do not carry us], downrushing, toward any true fact. We know *[desire
took delight]* but what took desire? Every night I tell you
[I am not someone who likes to wound] and you tell me you are
not someone who likes to wound. That we don't mean *[to
wound]*. And wound. And wound. Always the sound of
a sad wonder trumpet, on a Saturday, repeating what we are.

Dirt cheap art and the beggings
      of a continental blush and the ladies
all white in their marriages and mustard
      that comes in little jars and I am educated,
too, in the deep, festive tradition of never
      having enough. A billion is a thousand
times a million, didn't you know? Let's
      be autocratic. I know the bad parts
of the city to avoid, and the cities
      to avoid, and the man in the city I once
loved but don't anymore to avoid. Each
      hour I'm without you is inexcusable.
I may be sleeping elsewhere, in a nation
      that knows *pas de tout* of your reaching.
But I'm not without thought of you
      tonight, or the negotiating of all our
different properties: my egg yolk, your
      yellow. My jazz routine, your continuous
swing. Is this a love story for a man
      or a country and what's the difference
anyway? Plains I once had to myself
      and rolling hills and stars and little
general stores and porches and faces
      with oil marks, it's all provocative
and retrospective now, and before you
      know it you are someone else's baby.
Tonight I celebrate only what I accomplished
      today: remembering a thigh
in exact light and my allegiance to it. And an ass,
      which is round and then
un-round. And the small murmur of the streetlight
      that beckons me away at a late hour

to a place that says, *Alright. You are*
alight. And then I'm home.

Love is not an actual helmet. It is
fashionable. We wear it to feel heavy
with gold. This is why the future concerns me.
We have never loved
the world only the words
we used to describe it. There are too many
machines to teach
us sadness. In the Midwest, a groom uses the tick
of his watch to say *I do*. The bride kisses him
with an industrial fan.
Everyone seems happy. The sky is
too busy with a lemon tree to notice.
We all understand romantic neglect. We think
it's romantic. We furnish
our losses with an armchair and stove. We live
in them for years. If we get hungry we go
shooting for birds which only creates more loss.
We handle it like pros. We are mere
beings with mere musings and mere
murderous hearts. If we didn't
measure ourselves radiance by radiance
we'd mistake all these flashes for an atom bomb.
We'd bunker down in our basements and wait
for the president's tears
or for a stationary battery-operated horse
that says *This sway* to leave
or a single white breast:
the kind of thing to look at when you sit down to grieve.

Tie the ribbon around yourself and see
how long it holds. You are alive and have
just begun to wrestle. There are other ways
to fly. You're trying to marry human and
loss, trying to shape and peel the wound.
Find a place to house large things. The
walrus lost its hands to evolution, so it
taught itself to roll. Now, you hover over
the earth. You're barely. The ground did
soften and forgive and still, you're winter.
There's no shame in wanting to be useful
again. You yo-yo and furl. You dress in
other people's clothes. And the light? It
cannot tell you from a hermit or a
horsefly. Today in Manhattan, not a single
person died. How's that for hope? You
must understand the history of loss did
not begin with you. You've got to spit out
this thing that you chew and chew. To
hurt is a way to love, I thought you knew?

WHAT WE HAVE LOST

We left them in little silver factories, our breathings, and continued on
as things unliving and for a short while, as trees.
        And when we gathered
on the church steps we knew we'd be human again, as confirmed by our
drinkings, but missed the wrapped leaves and so swerved
        toward the bathtub
and were, for a day, droplings of bath water and tiny blond hairs. Imagine
it harder, our hybrid selves, both dirty and divine. Everything is
        a question of
belief: we began as bone bits and once we tired, we began again
as a two-lover herd. That time I was a real woman, I yearned for your square
        back of wanting, your yellow sun gut.
We are a thousand different shapes before we are the shapes we die in. If there
is a map for grief, it has already lost its world. Soon it will be a shower curtain
        or blueprint. Soon we'll be burning
it for warmth. I could love you more easily as a pale bird, circling you with air.
I would love you a lot more if you weren't so alive. We will always need
        things to teach us leaving;
there are a million kinds of loss. Each one has to do with breathing
        and not breathing.

Winnow

Blame the starfish, its triangle losses and gains. How fancy to lose
an arm these days. To let what's unwhole become whole and back again—
this is called swinging. Last night, I dreamt I was a lobster,
one-clawed and hardly. You, a four-sided constellation of the sea.
What choices we had: to complete ourselves, ourself. To imagine our broken
off parts in some marriage of their own. By morning, we'll know better.
We are not fancy. We must stick to the only wholeness we know:
to let what is missing stay missing. And swing? *No.*

A Deconstruction of Memory

If movements undo me, be waterbed, be scooter,
be my train leaving in the night. I'll be waiting
by the booth, my one squared escape. When
we're far away and sad, be umbrella, be hat,
be my ticket back home. Let's go someplace where
all the barns are yellow. Remember the grasslands.
Remember the splendor of ache and autonomy.
If I'm woman, be man, be full and daring.
The farmhouse did all it could and by 5 a.m.
the hay was ours, too. If movements undo me,
be horse, be cow, be the dragging of the loot.
I'll be wind rose, I'll be tumbleweed. I'll be
the leaving and the way we left. Remember
the last whistle, remember the zip of cars.
If sounds undo me, be *Aw,* be *Ow*, be the vibration
of skin. We're always late to that starved last
thought. And memory is such a heavy feather.
You said we couldn't go back. Oh ruffian, be wrong.

Rules of Leaving

an errata

Where I put *you* read *him*.
Where I put *a curve*

    in the road read *curve in your body,*

        curve of my face, in any skin
mine or yours.

    And if you see a bird fly by the window,
        know there was never any bird.

We are alone in the room.

    Where I put *room* read *bed* read *motel*
    read *the basement of the Laundromat.*

        And if I say this past Sunday,
    read *next Tuesday,*
    read *rain on the curve of the road,*

        dangerous conditions.

Your shirt on the chair will remain your shirt on the chair.

    Where I put *I don't love you anymore*
        read *I love you*   Pay attention.

Sunday, we are alone in the room.

    Your shirt hangs over the chair
        and I don't love you anymore.
A bird flies by the window.

What we learned most was to talk about weather:
Today there was a little sun and I saved it
as I would a sweet apple.
Destruction is everywhere;
I invented Zurich just to find you a safe place.
We wrap our legs around the years
in order to take them down.
That's the technology between us.
Etiquette says to kiss my hand first, then bring on
the wreckage. What is modern is being
able to say *I love you* with a mouse and map.
I once ruled
a state in love and lost all power.
There's no clear evolution.
August is almost over now,
it's hot and cold
at once. All I know is
we knocked each other over
to get here. Sadness and sobbing
were our only real clothes.
We lasted. We didn't last.
We chased each other's legs down the bed
until the end of light.
When we need the end, we'll invent it.
We are a pile of forgiving stars.
It will be behovely,
to leave you some place there is no weather.
No predications, just a chance.

TWO

REINVENTION

To be in the good world and as sore as you, a pity good lovin' brought us, no wits,

here.   Hubbubs and dingers are always blazonry in the first
place. These fits of fits: we are lousy   with imagining and the loveliest bits

of fucks still in us. Franken-lark Franken-sigh   monster of the beauteous,

        in spring we were

dulce and hot wired. It's fair to say made and made.   My jubilant caboose,
I beg you to end me

behind the Japanese honeysuckle. We'll move in sentences of this:

        the first phrase is forgetting the second phrase is forgetting the third phrase

Grief, you big egg we have no hard time for.
Let's take all this modern stuff and let it   beat: *nth* it goes *nth.*

Two little mouthfuls and a bang,
   no a *pang*, and this morning I fell
in love with a toaster oven
   and the way everything goes, eventually,
to the mouth. I once saw a ravenous
   cherub cry because his potatoes
were so goddamn beautiful he couldn't
   eat them. Of food, I'd kiss the oranges
blue. Of you, I'd forgotten what
   it's like to burst. We've said it so
many times: *We're hungry, we suffer.*
   But the turkey sat on the table
for three hours while we fucked
   and who's to say we were wrong?
If we weren't starving for one thing,
   we'd starve for another. We are American,
after all. If we weren't full of desire
   we would be German or Christian.
We'd close the fridge and look each other
   in the eye. When you're here I dream
of French words, Chinatown lanterns,
   paper-bagged lunches. When you're gone
I don't dream at all. The problem
   with food (and you) is that I keep finding
out that I'm human. But let's not think
   about logistics. I'm in love with you,
I'm in love with bread. I want to eat
   everything in sight. Here in this beautiful
muchness, we'll eat ourselves godly
   and full. Which will be exceptionally
historic, given our history of suffering.
   And tomorrow, don't say tomorrow.

Let's not be futuristic. We don't
know how long this will last.

Meditation in *B*

Birdbath out back but we are the birds of this tub,
our little boat almost sunk and us beneath it; necks
smeared with a pithy brightness. Let this

be a lesson in the syntax of bodies: soon between us
will be only sleep and sleeping things. Tell me
one is not yellow and buxom and beginning;

where's your sense of weightfulness? Things are all we are:
bits of borings and booms. But in sleep we are
in battery love: charging

and ready before. When you step out naked of the tub,
Je ne sais pas mon nom. We are close to bed now.
One late night snack. I'm butter

you're bread. We can be prison food, happily. And if
hungry is beautiful in any of these ways, I want to
eat I want to eat I want to eat it.

Two wrecks in a room: the beginning of every sorry-edged thought. Hand over all your possible languages and you won't get hurt. We go together like Mozart and sulfur. All this musical burning. *Red want.* What is it? It's something that you don't do which I cannot name. I miss it so much. It's set between us like a giant swan. I associate all thought with blushing. Thoughts of me. Of you. The big birch in the back wants to be the only one. Evenings are like this. Begging for their own perfect light. Part of my mind is always blowing, the other part is restless and trimmed. It's still cheap to want each other. If June wants to finish us we will always associate it with nostalgia: memory where the heart should be. All my wits to you in this final try. It's true that I will love your body more when I no longer have it. It will translate your stunning into something bearable. Too much beauty can break your neck.

Depends on what dwindles   (it all it all)
depends on the assemblage how we move
each other   (we are people we are
strangers)   I don't want to know what
that means. Some acts extinguish the
dream   (suitcases and shadow-plats and
trotting eyes in heads)   Beauty comes
before we are familiar with it and less after
(delight in anything that can move us
from our spaces) Your body is a place
(sometimes   a   thousand   places)
depending on how it's sold, bought. I
could love a man who never loved me
back so long as he has a map   (maps
last a long time longer than we're lasting)
The future is political   (it is a naked
girl)   we wait to let it thrill us but it
 never comes. The dream is a free machine
(the lever is one-winged)   if we fly out
we will dwindle. And for all that glowed
and all we knew then   (we wanted
each word to contain fading)   from
across the cement we illuminate our
history just to see where it starts (and
where it went).

Somehow, We are National

Whoever designed holes must've designed love
overnight in a brash moment
when someone who said they would occupy their mouth
didn't occupy their mouth
because they were out occupying Wall Street
or the rain or a pastrami sandwich on rye
and whoever said to dream this big must've thought
dreams want us back
they don't want us back
it's like we are businessmen in a garden
and the garden screams
get out of my beautiful space
so we wing it in our suits and walk to Wall Street
and for a moment all the people are a collective monument
and it is remarkable it slays us
and we can't be part of it because we are wearing suits
but we never asked to be businessmen
or to dream and we realize we love each other
but in the corporate sense
where one is a giant and the other a poor rat
and nothing is ever equal
and that is why love is a revolt
your bones are not magnificent they are bones
all we can do is hold our hands in the air
until we can't anymore
and watch out for holes in the street
and not get sucked in but sing to halcyon skies
and purple mountains and grace
your body is not a bell but let's swing it
your body is something to ring and I'll ring it.

Of Largeness

But what you meant by distance was globe,
was be mine, hushbug,
and we'll sleep the sleep of sky-
scrapers, grand blueprints
of built greatness—unrocked, unexploded,
half full of heaven and earth—
Expats to this homeflat, no longer
humbled to the bottommost bottom.
O America we never wanted
your size but here
it is and we can't contain ourselves:
modest travelers in a mammoth world.
What else to do but grow
into each other?
Let's drink to that.
Take a swig, darling, and turn
out the light.
Sometimes we have to beg
each other to be beautiful—drumming
and room-burnt.
Sometimes we just are.
Your knees are the end of a planet
I've shooked and shooked.
Roundest 360-degree-love I turn just to turn you.

CONJUGATED

Loved you as a humdinger
          in Chicago,
loved you muscle-ly in the long
bluster of winter. I to you, always
          is the way
to move—I to you recited in doorways
and driveways and archways. Anyway
          we could fit
together. We temper. Or we timber.
          However we bend
and burst, it's mighty. I've studied
          the body long
enough to know it's not a body
until it's been turned. The useful
          hand made useful
by the breast, the breast by the ass,
          ass by the last
useable limb. Your legs begging
          to be rammed
into the same dark structure as mine,
because the weather has said we can
          not leave
yet. Look at us: becoming unbecoming.
Us, with our costly hearts. We love, you
          have loved, I will love
you, stave by stave. Whatever we do now
          will be undone.
Damn the bus always leaving. Damn
          this besotted joy.
By the bridged river we wait in a window
for the last of snow to fall. Here is where
          we are, you have, I will

be fumbled and thrown. I saying to you,
　　　　you to I, *Oh come*
on honey, one last stand in my soul.

FRAGMENTS OF TIME

I want   to tell you how   it splits
me   how I am so sad for
what strays   you fix your hair   you leave
my chest   you say it's not
my   chest   I know   it's the ache of
another thing   I miss   the hordes
that count us   back   back
it's a fact   of the past   to want
to carry it all   forward   there   is
no sadder hour   than   the hour
I thought you said   *it's beautiful*
to be your longing   but you meant   it felt
even   longer   I'm told   I don't weep
correctly   I wish   you can't wish
time makes us   both sorry   we sound
like wings   when   we're sorry
which sounds like   shimmer and go
and go   all we've done since

Little crumbs and tree and bone
   and all that's left of time inside
our bodies, and I am insatiable
   when it comes to saving you,
my ally, my last wreckage of.
   It's business, this vanishing, to come
and go like little mice. We don't survive.
   Because of each other. We survive. Marriage
is a wilderness we must all come out
   of. Pull me from the poplar. Let's learn
to un-love like a million others. There
   are centuries surrounding us on both
sides: years of doom and dagger,
   years of *licht* and licked. And what we love
about time is what we love
   about failure: we can't stop it. It comes
toward us with both hands. It glows for us
   in the night. A wife tethered to a husband
tethered to a wife. We last, because we have
   lasted. Because leaving is the hardest way
to travel. It's brave to lose the part of you
   that can't be lost. To whittle a marriage down
to its bones and finally say *I want you*
   to be gone in the morning. Outside there's a kingdom
full entirely of newness. Inside we are two
   old gods. There's no space we can keep together.
In the rung, tough cold we'll kiss it all
   goodbye. And the bed will fight us
from across the room, where still we come,
   and breathe as we go: nth and nth and nth.

We are Mostly Merciful

Again, everything is difficult again. The newspaper says
the world is in no way merciful. So we must be
in no way merciful.
I rehearsed it all night—the absence of mercy,
as a condition to you who said
When I am in the same room as your body I am
           in a different room. There's nothing exquisite about lashing
a thing unless the thing is blazon with want.
The minor part of me thinks obsession is what kills
thinking. The major part thinks obsession makes the world
go round. By Sunday, the trees are still
gold outside the window and we think we are fine.
That the world collects good
light and is saving it for us. We can think it's mercy,
that a meteorite hit Russia
while we washed each other in the shower in California.
Or that death is only natural when it is
far away from us. No matter what's happening, mercy is
when I tell you *Stay, the field is full of stray horses,*
           or *Stay, your hair's so wet it could freeze.*
And you do, you stay, and collect all of your mercies
for me into one night. By morning, everything will be
difficult again. If a woman is bad, she can nuzzle
a horse's head and be forgiven. But if a man
is named Leningrad, we will only think of him as burning.
It's obsession that will never let us be good
to each other. It's mercy that will keep us
in the same room. The brightness through the window
and the lashing of our bodies is too difficult to rehearse.
No matter how hard we try we could never be news.
But the light was good for me, was it good for you?

A Meditation in Adverbs

Carefully

How we got here isn't as important as what we've become: ragged plums.
The hat you wear isn't the hat I gave you. The clock is broken. I wanted
you to move the bookcase. I wanted the dishes scrubbed. My wrist hurts.
The suitcase is packed. I've eaten enough of you now. When I told you
to touch me, I meant always and this way. Pain either needs to be explained
or it doesn't, like this.

Suddenly

When I was obsessed with physics, I'd take objects down from the attic
and drop them from the staircase: birdcage, doll, ukulele. You'd watch
the falling, ask me questions: *So the attic is empty now?* No, the objects are empty
because they have no home. *So the attic is full?* No, it's also empty. *Are we
the objects or the attic?* We are the falling. In marriage, nothing and everything
happens like this.

Nearly

Where are you little body? I was once fastened to you like a button. Please knock
on my door. The house, your ass—things I miss most or almost. There is a line
drawn across the bed. This is how I measured the small of your back against mine.
Also, there are measuring spoons in the kitchen, plenty of guilt. The recipe calls
for exactness. Oh how close we were to failing or not—like this.

Deliberately

Why we've gotten here isn't as important as how: once I was gold, then tin.

I changed elements depending on the light you'd switch on and off. When I was gold you'd call me sunbeam. When tin, you'd lock the bedroom door.

It's the space between want and action—this tizzy. To get to love take everything that is not love and drop it to the ground. Like this.

Where We Have Been

Alaska in the summer, married to the yellow bird's baby.
Around the mulberry bush you come shimmering, baby

of the disbanded North where Boötes walks the firmament,
dreaming of a smaller violence and happy-to-come babies.

From mulberry to meat, we are Canada fighting a more
southern Canada. Same government. Same army, baby.

But husband and wife soldiers move back to back around
the mono-city: the one called providence or complexity, baby.

Only bygone lovers traveling the world before us in
their wounded ships would wish to be more warless, baby.

French-bitten on all sides of your face you know it's love
that makes us fresh, egg-beaten, browbeaten babies.

And happy to go on this worldly jaunt, but only in Praha
could we drunkenly fool marriage into being holy, baby.

And no other wish but to last until Caroline Island and let's
be careful with this time, this map, this amalgamation, this baby.

Maybe east means end, maybe we're done and done, with lungs
the size of China, lovely to be tangled in your breathing, baby.

WOUND! OUT FROM BEHIND TWO CROUCHING
MASSES OF THE WORLD THE WORD LEAPT

Tuesdays are long and red. They're red because I've made them red. So you can see a color
in your mind
when you picture the dog. The dog walking across the yard. The oak. The space betwixt
and between
the dog and the oak. Now it can't be any other color. Even though grass is not red. Even
though there is
no grass. Or there is no yard at all and the dog trots into the street. Or there is no dog and
you must invent
one for yourself. And you will. Because Tuesdays are long and red. And if I tried to change
them to something
else now, I couldn't. Minds are minds. They do what you want them to. They obey like dogs.
Look. See. Know.
If I say the word over and over again it will sound like something new. A command. It will
come to mean
something like *Wipe your feet* or *Don't leave me yet.* Soon we'll be able to replace it with
other things
we've learned. Yolk. Log. The distance between two alike things. The distance between two
unalike things.
The decision I must make now. Whether or not we are fastened together like moth wings or
clam shells. Whether
we hurt. And what is symmetry anyway but two things wanting, in all their possible differences,
to be exactly
the same? I tell you Tuesdays are long because they are long in this deciding. And red, so you'd
have something
to look at while I think this through: how to know if we are these two, tightly wound things, or just
a wound plus a wound?

after Anne Carson

A Reconstruction of Memory

If only we weren't a war, a history
I must keep. Then I'd work
my way through our ages, take the good
years and spill them
out on the floor in front of us:
here's where the doctors
were wrong, here's where our room
became a factory
of sighs. There were
flowerpots, gravitas, skies
the color of bruises. A man
in the alley that sang: *Stay, bug, stay.*
All these things were ours.
We found them in the centrifuge,
the spinning jet.
Even the rinds, even the spires tell
we've been pulled and curled.
There was east coast, lamp posts, clocks
the shape of the earth.
There was light everywhere.
Where are those days we swore
we'd never lose?
Grief is the machine
that let's us keep each other forever.

Rules of Becoming
a revision

What was yellow is now blue. And what was blue is now
water is now rain, a puddle, a black shoe. Tell me nothing
can change. All things change. The flower in my hand is
a bird, a sparrow, a gray sparrow, a stone.
There is no logic really. The apple becomes a starfish,
the bell a glass of wine.

What we'll always have becomes something we lost,
becomes something we want, becomes sadness.
There is a better ending. Now the wine has turned.
Your body holds like a stone—
inside it's light, it's yellow.

The First Marriage

One thing is kind to another thing when both things are wounded. It's planetary how
            it starts. Lover there's a little sea,
little sky, and a large landmass for reckoning. It's routine. It doesn't taste like berries
            or a carafe of glass.
There is an abandoned zeppelin somewhere off the bridge. You can't trust a world
            with sky in every direction.
One thing is cruel to another thing when both things are wounded. It's all flick and flack.
            Once birds were the way we imagined
ourselves leaving. Lovers hemmed me up so I'd fit in the world and now I am too small.
            Keep spinning me good
so my atoms stay intact. The buildings demonstrate it every day, like so, like so. It's far
            too easy to come apart.
How do I make you happy when we are half born to fail and half to run wild through
            an unholy earth? I carry you
more and more. One thing is kind to another thing when both things are wounded.
            When you're a wobbly horse, I am
a wobbly horse. When you're thirsty, I am thirsty. When you're headed toward the future,
            I'll be holding you
back. Little bumps, we caress you as our own. We've taken the last shuttle and have been
            barefoot in the station for what
seems like years. The signs say we'll ache upon arrival. The signs say we must gently burn
            as we board. One thing is cruel
to another thing when both things are wounded. Once we borrowed some vintage wings
            and flew back toward a guttural machine.
When we couldn't stop, we let it suck us toward the rooster house into a rattling coup.
            At first the birds were startled. They let us
have our bodies into the night. By morning we were pecked into small broken pieces,
            for the first time proper lovers.
We lived like this for years, inside the same gray hen, whispering between rib and gall,
            Oh marry me in the minor light.
One thing is kind to another thing when both things are wounded. The hen got tired
            of our breathing and for days she wretched

and wretched until we dropped down, one single egg to warm and herry. She loved on us
           for weeks, warming our shell
with her soft bottom. This is how we learned intentional closeness, sinew to sinew, near the
           end of the world. As the sky darkened
she took our egg in her claw and flew off with it toward a heavier blue. Everything is not in
           its right place. There's nothing to circle, nothing
to save, no way to be only kind or only cruel. We don't need disaster to teach us ruin; the earth
           is blazing with hurt all over. We were fine
inside that egg, one yolk to get us through. Then with a squawk and flap, she said *I-love-you-*
           god-speed and cracked us in two.

[the opposite is cured with the opposite]

Gratitude to the editors and staff of the following journals who published these poems, sometimes in earlier versions:

Anti: *"A Deconstruction of Memory"*
The Awl: *"To Grieve, in Other Verbs"*
Barrelhouse: *"Epithalamium ABC," "Rules of Leaving"*
Barn Owl Review: *"Where We Have Been"*
Best New Poets Anthology 2011: *"Conjugated"*
Black Warrior Review: *"Conjugating"*
Bodega Magazine: *"The Function of You and I"*
Boston Review: *"The First Marriage"*
Boxcar Poetry Review: *"Rules of Becoming"*
The Brooklyn Review: *"A Meditation in Adverbs"*
Cell Poems: *"Of Newness"*
Colorado Review: *"Heroic Sentences"*
Columbia: A Journal of Literature and Art: *"Invention"*
Columbia Poetry Review: *"What We Have Lost"*
DIAGRAM: *"Winnow"*
Guernica: *"Of Largeness"*
Gulf Coast: *"Somehow, We are National"*
inter|rupture: *"Reinvention"*
The Kenyon Review: *"We Are Mostly Merciful"*
Linebreak: *"Conditional Dreaming," "Reverie," "Meditation in B," "Modern Sentences"*
Quarterly West: *"We Are Mostly Alright"*
The Southern Review: *"Wound! Out from Behind Two Crouching Masses of the World the Word Leapt," "Somehow, We are a We"*
TriQuarterly: *"The Functions of X and Y"*
Two Weeks: An Anthology of Contemporary Poetry: *"American Sentences"*
Washington Square Review: *"Hunger Sentences"*

"Heroic Sentences" was republished on Poetry Daily
"Somehow, We are a We" and *"Conjugating"* were republished on Verse Daily

The italicized excerpts in "Fragments of Sappho" (p.14) are from *If Not, Winter: Fragments of Sappho* (Knopf, 2002), translated by Anne Carson.

I'm very grateful to the Creative Writing Program at Stanford University who awarded me a Wallace Stegner Fellowship to complete this book. Thank you to all the Stegner Fellows and lecturers for their support of my work. Gratitude to all of my wonderful teachers, especially Eavan Boland, Ken Fields, Simone Di Piero, D.A. Powell, Stephen Dunn, BJ Ward, Peter Murphy, and Svea Barrett. And to all of my lovely students who teach me everyday.

Thank you to Allison Davis and Meghan Privitello, who read this book and helped shape it into its best possible form.

Thank you to Gabriel Fried and the Lexi Rudnitsky Project for believing in this work.

Thank you to my parents, my entire family, and all of my friends for supporting everything I do.

Thank you to John, for being my other half.

Finally, for my beautiful Grandmother Turtle, my first fan.

And for my late friend Etta Chinskey, a wonderful poet who championed this book before anyone else did. This book is for you.